Elizabeth Ripley

TITIAN

BIOGRAPHIES BY ELIZABETH RIPLEY

TITIAN

A Biography by

ELIZABETH RIPLEY

OXFORD UNIVERSITY PRESS

London

ILLUSTRATIONS

TITIAN and his brother walked down a wooded path leading from their house to the river. They paused to look out at the snow-capped mountains pink from the glow of the rising sun. They would not see the woods and hills of Cadore again, for they were on their way to Venice to learn a trade.

They were eager to see that island city built in water where people traveled by boat instead of horseback, where the marble palaces looked like lace and the churches were lined with pictures made of little pieces of glass. Titian and his brother were going to learn how to make these mosaic pictures in Master Zuccato's workshop.

The mountain air had agreed with Gregorio Vecellio's two sons. They were strong, sturdy boys. Titian at nine was almost as tall as eleven-year-old Francesco. It was time for them to earn a living. Money was scarce in the little village of Cadore, but Venice in 1496 was the richest seaport in Italy. The artists' workshops were busy turning out pictures for churches and palaces. The great painter Bellini even received a lifetime salary for painting portraits of each Doge, or governor of Venice.

Titian had not been in Zuccato's workshop long before his master decided that the boy should study painting in Bellini's studio. It was exciting to work in glowing oil colors, trying to capture the effect of lustrous silk and of shimmering light on water.

The boy was not yet twenty when he received his first commission. Jacopo Pesaro, bishop and soldier, was about to command the Venetian fleet in a war against the Turks. He wanted a picture of himself praying for victory before Saint Peter. Titian painted his important patron in bishop's robes, his helmet by his side. The Pope who had placed the Bishop in command stood behind him, and in the background was a blue lagoon filled with warships.

Votive Picture of Jacopo Pesaro

About 1506. (57½" x 72¼")

ROYAL MUSEUM OF FINE ARTS, ANTWERP

Venetians passing up and down the Grand Canal in 1507 stopped to look at the picture the artist Giorgione was painting above a door of the German warehouse. They compared it with the picture which a young artist from Cadore was painting above another door. Some decided that Titian's figure of Justice trampling on a head was more impressive than the older artist's graceful nudes. Giorgione, seeing the figure come to life, wondered if his young assistant had surpassed him. He had met the country boy at Bellini's studio, and had noticed that Titian's vigorous figures looked as if they were alive. He was impressed by the Hercules the boy had painted over a palace door, and decided to hire him to help with his warehouse paintings.

When the warehouse paintings were finished, Titian's name had become well known in Venice, but there were few commissions for any artist in the spring of 1508, for Emperor Maximilian was threatening to invade Italy. Already his army was marching across the mountains from Austria. After a valiant fight the fortress of Cadore surrendered, and Venice sued for peace. These were lean days for artists. Some sought work in Rome, and Titian set off for Padua to paint frescoes in a church.

Titian's pictures showed miracles of Saint Anthony. In one the patron saint of Padua healed a man who had cut off his own leg because he kicked his mother. In the background Titian painted the mountain fortress of Cadore against a sunset sky, but when the colors were brushed into the wet plaster they did not glow like the oil paints he had used in Venice. Titian worked on the paintings for two years. Then he sent a generous portion of his earnings to his family in Cadore, and returned to Venice.

Plague had swept through the city while Titian was in Padua. His partner had not been spared. Giorgione had died, leaving many unfinished canvases. Titian was commissioned to complete the pictures. He was glad to be working in shiny oils once more. He was glad, too, that his name had not been forgotten. Soon the young artist from Cadore was receiving commissions of his own.

8

Saint Anthony Healing a Youth's Leg

1511.

SCUOLA DEL SANTO, PADUA. PHOTO ANDERSON

The monks of Santo Spirito, who had prayed fervently that the plague might end, wished to express their thanks to the saint who had saved their city. They commissioned Titian to paint an altarpiece dedicated to this patron saint of Venice. Titian placed a bearded model in a bright blue robe on a pedestal and arranged the folds of a red mantle across his knees. This was Saint Mark sitting enthroned against a radiant sky. Below stood the saints who were protectors from the plague: on one side Saint Cosmo and Saint Damian in red doctor's robes, and on the other the martyrs Saint Roch and Saint Sebastian.

Visitors from abroad marveled at the new painting in the church of Santo Spirito which brought warm rich light to the dark space above the altar. A cardinal from Rome urged Titian to visit the Holy City, where he could win money and fame working for the Pope. But Titian preferred to stay in Venice. Bellini was growing old. Soon the government would choose another artist to paint pictures for the council hall. Titian's friends urged him to send a petition to the city council.

"I, Titian of Cadore," he wrote in the spring of 1513, "desirous of fame rather than profit wish to serve the Doge... rather than ... the Pope... I am therefor anxious to paint in the Council Hall... a canvas of the battle on the same conditions as are conceded to Bellini." The Council did not delay to send their answer:

"Prepare for the said Titian all... he demands..." the council ordered. He would have a salary, two assistants, and a studio in San Samuele, the busiest section of Venice.

Titian made a drawing of a battle scene and imagined how it would look painted in glowing colors lighting up the dark corner of the council hall. He wondered if Bellini had told the council to give him this unimportant space. He knew that the old master was jealous of his former pupil, but he did not know that Bellini was urging the council to cancel his rival's salary.

The battle was only a rough sketch on canvas when, in the spring of 1514, Titian was summoned to the Doge's Palace.

Saint Mark Enthroned

About 1511. (89" x 57¾")

SANTA MARIA DELLA SALUTE, VENICE. PHOTO ANDERSON

Titian was stunned when he heard the government's order read before the council. How could he support his new wife without the government salary, and how could he finish the battle scene without the help of his assistants? He had already taken on other commissions for private patrons. His workshop was filled with unfinished canvases.

He placed one of these canvases on his easel as soon as he returned to San Samuele. It was a romantic scene like the ones Giorgione used to paint; figures in a shadowy landscape pictured the three ages of man. Three sleepy cupids, gathered round a tree trunk, represented childhood; a pair of lovers, symbolizing youth, were seated in the foreground; and old age, a bearded man holding two skulls, sat on a distant hillside. Titian brushed in leafy trees against a stormy sky, strengthened the lights and shadows on the young man's figure, and smoothed over the delicate shadings of the girl's flesh tones. Then he turned the painting to the wall and placed another canvas on his easel. The gentleman from Faenza would have to wait, while he finished a *Sleeping Venus* for Alfonso d'Este of Ferrara. He was tired of those visits from Duke Alfonso's secretary, inquiring about the pictures ordered by his master. As soon as they were ready he would bring them to Ferrara, he wrote Alfonso.

He must make every effort to please this important client. The Este family were rich and powerful and enthusiastic patrons of the arts. He was proud that his paintings would be hanging in Alfonso's study with pictures by Italy's greatest artists. He picked up his brush and painted with renewed vigor.

The battle scene stayed where it was, turned to the wall in a corner of his studio. There it would stay until Titian received an answer from his new petition asking for renewal of his salary. The council met, debated, but came to no decision.

From Alfonso came impatient letters. The Duke wanted to see his pictures. Titian put the last touches on the *Sleeping Venus,* packed up the other canvases, and set off for Ferrara.

12

The Three Ages of Man

About 1515. (42" x 72")

EARL OF ELLESMERE COLLECTION, ON LOAN TO THE
NATIONAL GALLERY OF SCOTLAND, EDINBURGH

Alfonso showed his visitor around his castle, talking enthusiastically about his treasures. In the evening Titian, dressed in his best, sat at the Duke's banquet table. He talked with poets, scholars, and musicians who were anxious to have their portraits painted by the famous Venetian artist. The Duke showered him with commissions which Titian promised to fill in his Venice workshop; but when he returned to San Samuele he had to attend to more important matters.

In the spring of 1516 Giovanni Bellini died. Titian of Cadore was appointed painter to the Doge. In payment for the *Battle* and for portraits of each new Doge he would receive a yearly salary. He dragged the battle scene from its corner, but it stayed untouched. A bigger canvas filled the center of the studio, covered by a scaffolding reaching to the ceiling. Father German, guardian of the Frari church, called often to inquire about the progress of this altarpiece he had commissioned. Through the openings in the scaffolding he saw spots of glowing color. He was eager to see the finished picture in the carved marble frame he had already ordered.

Two years later Titian's *Assumption* was carried to the Frari church and placed in its frame above the altar. Light seemed to shine from the spot where it was hanging. The Virgin, draped in brilliant red, stood on a bank of luminous clouds. Below were apostles, arms outstretched, their faces turned toward heaven. Father German shook his head. He had never seen such strangely proportioned figures, drawn as if they were looked at from below. The picture was too dramatic. He preferred the dignity of Bellini's paintings, but he decided to let the people of Venice see it.

One spring day in 1518 Father German watched and listened as thousands filed by the biggest altarpiece they had ever seen. They were staggered by the movement in the picture, and the colors shot through with brilliant light. Father German began to change his mind. He would not sell it to the Emperor's ambassador, who had asked to buy it. Already the painting had brought glory to his church, and the artist was now the most talked of painter in all Italy.

14

The Assumption of the Virgin

1516–1518. (272″ x 142″)

BY COURTESY OF THE BASILICA DI S. MARIA GLORIOSA DEI FRARI

Alfonso's faithful secretary, Tebaldi, continued to call at the San Samuele studio. Now that the *Assumption* was finished, he reported to his master, Titian had more time to work on the Duke's pictures. He was finishing a small wood panel for the door of Alfonso's study. The picture illustrated a quotation from the Bible which Alfonso had chosen for his family motto: "Render unto Caesar the things that are Caesar's." These were Christ's words when He refused the coin offered Him by a Pharisee. Tebaldi admired the carefully painted folds of Christ's red tunic and blue cloak, and the subtle shading of His face and hands which contrasted with the Pharisee's swarthy flesh tones. But Titian was not satisfied. He picked up a small brush and drew each strand of Christ's hair and beard. He would show those Germans who had criticized his broad brush strokes that he could paint as precisely as their great Dürer. The Duke would have his picture after he had perfected every detail.

Alfonso waited. *The Tribute Money* was left to dry, while Titian started an altarpiece for the Pope's ambassador. The council reminded him that they were waiting for the *Battle*. They threatened to hire another artist if Titian did not produce the picture. He depended more than ever on his salary, now that he had a baby son, but he must not displease the impatient Duke.

In the fall of 1519 Titian arrived in Ferrara. The energetic Duke rushed him from one project to another. A damaged painting must be restored, a special balcony designed. Titian must advise him on new ways to fire pottery, and one day he sent the artist off to sketch a strange gazelle which had been seen near Venice.

Titian did not linger in the Duke's luxurious court, for the Pope's ambassador was waiting for his altarpiece. Alfonso's commissions would be filled in the San Samuele studio. Paints and canvases were loaded on a boat. Titian said good-by to Alfonso and sailed down the river Po to Venice.

16

The Tribute Money

About 1518. (28⅞" x 22")

GEMALDEGALERIE, DRESDEN. PHOTO ALINARI

"Make it your business to speak with Titian," Alfonso wrote Tebaldi, "and remind him that he made promises he has not thought fit to keep." He had waited long enough for the *Bacchus and Ariadne* he had ordered for his study. He was tired of hearing about the altarpiece for the Pope's ambassador which occupied the artist's time. If Titian was so proud of that figure of Saint Sebastian in the side panel, would Tebaldi please buy it for his master? Titian hesitated, then refused the offer. He could not offend the Pope's ambassador.

Alfonso wrote again: "Let him know," he told Tebaldi, "that we have thought the matter over... and resolved that we shall not do this injury to the Reverend Legate."

Two years went by before Alfonso saw the promised painting. Tebaldi continued to report from Venice. Now that the altarpiece was finished, Titian spent his mornings working on the *Battle*. As soon as the Duke sent him more paints he would finish the *Bacchus and Ariadne*. He knew that the picture would please his master, who loved scenes from Greek mythology. Bacchus, was leaping from his chariot to greet the startled Ariadne. His silver-red cloak made a dramatic splash of color against the deep blue sky. Ariadne in a bright blue mantle turned toward Bacchus, holding up her arm in amazement. A noisy group of nymphs and satyrs danced behind the chariot.

In the winter of 1523 Titian's assistants loaded Alfonso's canvases on a boat and sailed up the river to Ferrara. Titian sent word that he would follow after a short visit to Mantua where he would visit Alfonso's nephew, Gonzaga. The Duke need not worry that he would accept commissions from Gonzaga, although he, like his uncle, was eager to have a Titian canvas. Titian would be loyal to His Excellency the Duke, whom he had promised faithfully to serve.

18

Bacchus and Ariadne

1523. (69" x 75")

NATIONAL GALLERY, LONDON. PHOTO ANDERSON

Titian kept his promise. He accepted no commissions from Alfonso's nephew. He would serve Gonzaga after his uncle's paintings had been finished.

The *Bacchus and Ariadne* was already hanging in the Duke's study when Titian arrived in Ferrara, and *The Tribute Money* was framed in a panel of a closet door. Alfonso followed Titian around the room, pointing to his favorite canvases. There was Bellini's lovely woodland scene which Titian had finished after his master grew too old to paint, and here was Alfonso's portrait which Titian had painted seven years before. The Duke wanted another picture of himself wearing a fur-trimmed black coat and a crimson velvet tunic with gold-brocaded sleeves. This time his hand would be resting on a cannon. He was proud that he had worked in a cannon foundry when he was young, although his family had not approved. Did Titian know that he had been a carpenter, too, and an assistant to a potter?

As the Duke talked, Titian studied the subject he was about to paint. He must capture the alert expression of his face and hands before Alfonso started him on any new commissions. The rest could wait until he returned to San Samuele.

Titian did not know that another important client was waiting to shower him with commissions when he returned to Venice. While he was in Ferrara the Doge had died. A new Doge had been elected and was waiting to have his portrait painted. Titian had to put aside Alfonso's paintings in order to perform his official duties for the government.

20

Duke Alfonso d'Este of Ferrara

About 1522. (50" x 38⅜")

METROPOLITAN MUSEUM OF ART, NEW YORK. MUNSEY FUND, 1927

Titian painted a half-length portrait of the Doge, his face framed by a white beard and his hand holding up the folds of his gold-brocaded cloak. He had painted the ducal robes before when he worked in Bellini's studio, but this time he did not show the pointed ducal cap in profile, because he was more interested in showing the expression of his sitter's strong, stern face.

As soon as the portrait was hung beside portraits of the other Doges in the council hall, Doge Gritti commissioned Titian to paint a picture of Saint Christopher at the foot of the stairway leading to his private chapel. This was in gratitude for the recent victory over the Emperor's army at the town of Saint Christopher.

Titian wondered if his picture would light up the dark space above the doorway. Not since Padua had he painted on wet plaster, and then the colors were dull and disappointing.

Every morning after Mass the Doge stopped at the foot of the stairway to admire Titian's picture. He was impressed by the vigorous figure wading through the waters surrounding Venice, and was charmed by the lovely Christ child on the saint's shoulders. It did not matter that the saint's blue tunic and red cloak lacked the luster he had seen in Titian's other paintings. He would ask this artist to decorate his chapel.

All through one steaming summer Titian labored in the ducal chapel. He never found time to finish Alfonso's paintings, or the portrait for Gonzaga, who had just presented him with a handsome doublet. He decided to put the finishing touches on that portrait.

When Tebaldi called at San Samuele, he found a pale and haggard Titian. Heat, hard work, and fever had laid him low. If he could persuade his doctor to recommend a change of air, perhaps the government would allow him to make a visit to Ferrara.

Alfonso waited hopefully. Fall came with crisp cool air to relieve the sweltering city. Titian's health improved. Soon he was hard at work finishing the ducal chapel. Alfonso could wait no longer. He ordered Tebaldi to hire a private barge to bring the artist and his pictures to Ferrara.

22

Saint Christopher

About 1523. (118" x 70½")

DOGE'S PALACE, VENICE. PHOTO ANDERSON

Alfonso tried desperately to keep Titian in Ferrara. He asked him to send to Venice for more colors so that he could paint portraits of members of the court. But the Duke could not keep his artist long. The Doge's chapel was still unfinished, and Titian wanted to visit Mantua before he returned to Venice.

Gonzaga was as persistent as his uncle in his attempts to attract the Venetian artist to his court. Titian had been impressed by Mantua's luxurious palace, filled with pictures by Italy's great artists, and by the attractive young Duke, who could well afford to settle a pension on Titian's young son, Pomponio. Here was an important patron who must be satisfied.

Titian returned to Venice with a crateful of unfinished canvases commissioned by Gonzaga. He had promised the Duke he would send *The Entombment* soon. Each day after he returned from the Doge's chapel he attacked the canvas with vigor. The rich, shiny oils glowed with a new brilliance as he played strong lights against the darks. He cast light on the body of the dead Christ so that the white, translucent flesh contrasted with the dark skin of the fisherman who held his master's legs. A brilliant light illuminated the silvery-red tunic of the man supporting Jesus's shoulders, and the anguished face of young Saint John, who held Christ's limp hand. Light played on the faces of Mary Magdalene and the grieving Virgin. Then, fearing that Jesus's tragic face looked too dramatic, Titian cast a deep shadow over the head and shoulders of the martyred Christ. As soon as the last coat of varnish had dried, he shipped the painting to Gonzaga. Now he would have time to finish the Doge's chapel.

24

Almost every day Doge Gritti trudged up the stairs to look at Titian's paintings. He grew to like this hard-working artist who had postponed commissions from important clients in order to serve the government of Venice. Now that the chapel was almost finished, he decided to award a judgeship to the artist's brother-in-law and find a good job for Titian's aging father. Gregorio Vecellio, the valiant soldier who had fought the imperial army in Cadore, was appointed inspector of the Cadore mines.

The Entombment

About 1527. (58¾" x 84¾")
LOUVRE, PARIS. PHOTO ALINARI

Thirteen years had passed since Jacapo Pesaro had returned victorious from his campaign against the Turks. He had changed little since Titian had painted him kneeling in prayer before Saint Peter. If that painting had brought him the victory he had prayed for, he must order another picture, as big and majestic as the *Assumption*, to hang in the Frari church. The canvas must be large enough to show him with members of his family kneeling before the Virgin's throne. It must include a turbaned Turkish prisoner and an armored knight holding the Pesaro family banner. Saint Peter would be standing at the Virgin's feet, and somewhere Titian must find room for Saint Francis and Saint Anthony.

Titian set to work making portrait sketches of members of the Pesaro family, then blocked out a composition on his canvas. He placed the figures inside a lofty church. The Bishop knelt before the Virgin's throne, his family on the other side. Pesaro was pleased with what he saw, although it was only a sketch in tones of brown. His eyes followed the grand, sweeping line leading from his hands, through Saint Peter's to those of the Virgin and the Christ child.

In between trips to Mantua and Ferrara and visits to the Doge's chapel, Titian would work on a face or a piece of drapery. The unfinished canvas stood in his studio for six years, but when, at last, the Doge's chapel was completed, Titian climbed the scaffolding in front of the Pesaro altarpiece and started to paint.

The figures looked overpowered by the massive archways of the church. He decided to paint a new background. Suddenly the walls became two columns soaring against an azure sky, and the ceiling a cloud on which were two cherubs holding up a cross.

One winter day in 1525 the Pesaro family gathered in front of an altar in the Frari church. When the curtain covering the altarpiece was drawn aside a warm rich light flooded the tiny chapel. Titian's canvas, like the *Assumption*, which hung nearby, was a masterpiece of glowing color.

Madonna of the Pesaro Family

1519–26. (191" x 106½")

Titian wished that he had more time to work on Pietro Aretino's portrait. Ever since the Doge's architect, ugly, red-haired Sansovino, had brought his noisy friend to San Samuele, Titian had wanted to paint his portrait. He liked this boisterous, aggressive writer who offered to advertise his pictures. Titian knew the power of Aretino's acid pen. Princes and cardinals had paid him to praise them in his poetry. He knew that a portrait of Aretino would please the Duke of Mantua, especially if accompanied by one of Aretino's brilliant letters. His reward might be that pension for Pomponio.

Gonzaga wrote enthusiastically to Aretino: "Be good enough to thank Titian in my name....I shall soon show him the gratitude I feel for so kind a demonstration."

Aretino's letters brought a flood of orders. Back and forth Titian traveled between Mantua and Ferrara, returning when he could to Venice. He started another altarpiece for the church of Saints John and Paul. As he enlarged the rough sketch he had submitted to the priests, he thought of how bitter his friend Pordenone had become because his careful drawings had not been chosen. But the priests believed that Titian's sketch would make a dramatic painting. It showed Saint Peter Martyr pursued by his assassin. His companion had fallen to the ground. On the same page Titian made another sketch. The companion fled in terror. The saint, who had fallen to the ground, pointed to two angels who appeared in a blaze of light above him. This was the picture which Titian painted in glowing colors. When it was hung in the church of Saints John and Paul, Pordenone listened to the praises heaped upon his rival's painting. Even the great Michelangelo, just arrived in Venice, admired the vigor of the figures and the brilliance of the colors. In despair Pordenone left for Rome.

Three hundred years later flames from the altar candles caught the dry brittle canvas and the famous altarpiece was destroyed. The picture which hangs in the church today is only a copy of one of Titian's masterpieces.

28

Sketch for Saint Peter Martyr

About 1527. (67" x 67")

CABINET DES DESSINS, LOUVRE, PARIS

The summer of 1530 was hot and sultry. Titian found it hard to work in his crowded studio. The noises from the canal annoyed him, and he was worried about his wife, who had caught a fever. He could hardly wait to move into the house he had rented in the suburbs. He liked to think of Pomponio playing with his little brother in the garden overlooking the lagoon. He would hire a nurse to care for his baby girl. Rest and quiet would soon cure Cecelia's fever.

Cecelia Vecellio did not live to breathe the clean air of Biri Grande. In August, Gonzaga's secretary wrote from Venice; "Our master Titian is quite disconsolate at the loss of his wife whom he buried yesterday."

From Cadore came Titian's sister Orsa to care for the busy household. But Titian could not bring himself to paint.

"I have such an irritation of the skin I cannot move," he wrote Gonzaga, but he told Gonzaga's secretary that his chief worry was Pomponio. He had planned for his son to be a priest, but not a word had he heard about the pension offered by Gonzaga.

"Titian's illness comes more from his melancholy state of mind," the Duke's secretary wrote, and then reminded his master of the pension.

In the fall the Vecelli family moved to Biri Grande. From his studio window, Titian looked across the lagoon to the snow-capped mountains of Cadore. Here he could work in peace. He placed one of Gonzaga's unfinished canvases on an easel and started to paint. It was a charming scene. The Madonna sat on the ground; Saint Catharine knelt beside her, holding the Christ child in her arms. The baby reached for a white rabbit his mother held against her knee. In the background Titian painted the figure of a shepherd sitting with his flock. He brushed in a mass of leafy trees behind him and picked out bits of shining river winding to the sea. Then in the distance he showed the sharp peaks of the Cadore mountains against a sunset sky.

30

Madonna with the Rabbit

About 1530. (27¾" x 33")

LOUVRE, PARIS. PHOTO ALINARI

The Emperor looked tired, Titian thought as he sketched his long, thin face framed by an auburn beard. His heavy blue eyes were sad. He did not smile when he complimented Titian on the likeness he had painted. He wanted two portraits of himself, one in armor and the other in court dress with his hand resting on the head of his favorite dog. The imperial clothes would be brought to Titian's studio so that the artist could copy the engraving on the armor and the details of the fur-trimmed coat, gold necklace, sword, and dagger. He would expect to receive the portraits as soon as he returned to Spain.

Titian shipped the finished portraits to the Emperor soon after the painter returned to Venice. He wondered if Charles would like the paintings. Should a peasant from Cadore, no matter how good a painter, expect to receive the imperial favor? But he would not worry about the portraits. Many months would pass before he could have an answer from Barcelona. In the meantime other important clients were waiting for their pictures.

In the spring of 1533 the Emperor's ambassador delivered a letter to the house in Biri Grande. Titian's hands trembled as he unrolled the scroll. Emperor Charles V, the letter said, would pose for no other artist. Titian and his family were hereby raised to the rank of nobles, and the artist would now wear the sword, gold spurs, and chain of the Knight of the Golden Spur. Not since Bellini had an artist received so great an honor.

Orders from other monarchs poured into Titian's studio. Francis I sent a medal stamped with a picture of his head. From this medal Titian painted three portraits of the king and shipped them off to France. He worked long hours in his studio, attacking first one picture then another. Not until the servants lighted the lanterns in his garden did he lay aside his brushes. Then he hurried to put on his velvet jacket, gold chain, sword, and spurs so that he would be ready to receive his guests.

Charles V with a Dog

About 1533. (75½" x 43¾")
PRADO, MADRID. PHOTO ANDERSON

Gonzaga dashed off a note to Titian in the fall of 1532, asking him to come to Mantua. He was entertaining the Emperor at his court. His Imperial Highness had seen the Duke's gallery of paintings. He had admired *The Entombment*, had been charmed by the *Madonna with the Rabbit*, and what impressed him most was Titian's portrait of Gonzaga. He must have his own portrait painted by this talented Venetian artist. Gonzaga had no sooner sealed the letter than he decided to write another. He must make his message seem more urgent. The Emperor had only a few days to spend in Mantua, Titian must come at once, and would he please bring along a special kind of Venetian fish.

Gonzaga wrote in vain. Titian could not leave Biri Grande even for a commission from the Emperor. The portrait would have to wait. Soon the imperial court would be moving to Bologna. Aretino had written Cardinal de Medici, asking him to invite Titian to that city. In this way Titian could add two new patrons to his list.

Cardinal Ippolito de Medici, like many other members of his family, was a lover of the arts. He was a politician, too. The Emperor would not forget that it was thanks to the Cardinal that Titian was coming to Bologna. He would have little time for sittings, but while he was busy with affairs of state the Cardinal would have his own portrait painted. Titian would love to paint the shimmering lights in the Hungarian officer's uniform that the Cardinal had worn in the campaign against the Turks. He tried on the plum-colored velvet jacket and the red cap topped by two dashing plumes. This was the costume he would wear. Titian would show him, not as a cardinal, but as a soldier holding a mace in one hand and a scimitar in the other.

It did not take Titian long to paint Ippolito's uniform, and it looked as rich and lustrous as the Cardinal had expected. But Titian was more interested in his sitter's lean, bearded face and the astute expression in his dark eyes, thin nose, and firm, straight mouth. Already he had grown to like and understand his newest patron.

Cardinal Ippolito de Medici

1533. (52½" x 42")

PITTI GALLERY, FLORENCE. PHOTO ALINARI

A canvas twelve feet high and twenty-five feet long filled one end of Titian's studio. How would he find time to paint this enormous picture for the school of Santa Carita, when he was constantly bothered by his other patrons? The ambassador from Mantua wanted to know about the medallion portraits of twelve Caesars, and the Duke of Urbino's secretary was always inquiring about his master's pictures. Ippolito de Medici urged him to come to Rome, and the Emperor urged him to visit Spain. At least he was spared those visits from Tebaldi. It had been a shock to learn of Alfonso's death. He would miss his good friend and oldest patron, but there would be more time for other work. As soon as his assistants transferred his sketch of the *Presentation of the Virgin* to canvas, he would start on the picture for the school's assembly hall.

It had not been easy to arrange so many figures on a canvas which would be pierced by two large doors, but Titian was pleased with the composition.

Halfway up a flight of stairs stood a little girl in blue surrounded by a halo of golden light. She stretched out her hand toward the priest who waited at the top. At the foot stood her mother, dressed in yellow. Her companion, in brilliant red, pointed to the Virgin. Behind them was a motley crowd such as Titian had often seen in Venice; senators in black robes and caps, a nobleman in brilliant red, a mother in gray her baby in her arms, begging for money. Another mother, half hidden by a monk in yellow, held the hand of her little girl, who was playing with a dog. The white headdress of a peasant woman, who sat with a basket of eggs in the foreground, made a splash of light against the gray stone steps.

Shifting lights playing over the marble palaces lining the street picked out bits of color in the costumes of the people leaning from the windows. Then, as a note of peace in this busy scene, Titian painted in the distance a view of the Cadore mountains, blue against a transparent sky.

The Presentation of the Virgin

1534–38. (136" x 295")

ACCADEMIA, VENICE. PHOTO ALINARI

Four years went by before *The Presentation of the Virgin* was ready to hang in the school of Santa Carita. They had been busy years for Titian. He filled orders for rich patrons who offered big rewards and then forgot to pay him. Even the Emperor had to be reminded of the pension he had promised. Busy as he was, Titian decided to join the imperial court in Asti. When he returned a few months later he had procured a pension for himself, one for Aretino and a priesthood for Pomponio.

But life was not cheap in Biri Grande. Assistants must be paid, materials bought, and important visitors entertained. The pension money was not enough. In despair he wrote to Gonzaga asking for his money. "I beg, I supplicate your excellency," he pleaded.

Only in Cadore did Titian forget his worries. Every summer he left the stifling city to get a breath of clear mountain air, but as soon as he returned to Venice creditors pursued him.

Then one day in 1537 a messenger from the government knocked on Titian's door and ordered the artist to appear before the council. For twenty-one years, he was told, he had received a salary, "on condition that he paint the canvas of the land fight." He had not fulfilled his promise. He was hereby ordered to refund all the money he had received. This was a staggering blow. He could not refund the money.

As soon as he returned to Biri Grande, he made quick sketches of a battle scene, not the Battle of Spoleto, ordered by the government, but the Battle of Cadore. The Venetian troops galloped across a bridge in pursuit of the Emperor's army, which fled up a hillside toward a flaming fortress. Then he put a fresh canvas on his easel and started furiously to work.

One year later the painting was placed beside the other battle scenes in the council hall.

"[It] is considered the best...and most beautiful in the hall," one critic wrote.

Forty years later fire broke out in the council hall and destroyed this famous painting.

38

Drawing of the Battle of Cadore

About 1538. (5⅛" x 7⅛")

CABINET DES DESSINS, LOUVRE, PARIS

Gonzaga wrote enthusiastically about the Caesar portrait just received from Venice. Would Titian please bring the others soon? He was anxious to see the twelve medallions in a frieze around his room. Titian shipped off three more Caesars with a letter to Gonzaga. The Duke of Urbino was very ill, he wrote. Titian had promised to join him in Pesaro. He would come to Mantua later. The sea air of Pesaro did not cure Urbino's case of poisoning. He died in agony a few weeks later.

When Titian returned to Venice, he accepted a commission to paint a portrait of General d'Avalos, Governor of Milan and ambassador from the Emperor. Here was his chance to ask about Pomponio's pension. Again his trip to Mantua had to be postponed.

D'Avalos listened sympathetically. He would speak to the Emperor about the pension. Titian could send the finished portrait to Milan. D'Avalos would send him a portrait of his son so that Titian could show him beside his father. His troops must be massed below him, listening attentively to his speech.

A few weeks later Titian received the pension money, but the Governor's portrait remained untouched. Titian had set to work on the Caesar portraits, while Aretino sent off diplomatic letters to Milan. The picture was progressing nicely, he told the General.

A year later Aretino wrote to Milan again. Titian had been called to Mantua to attend Gonzaga's funeral. His good friend and patron never saw the Caesar portraits.

The General's picture would soon be ready, Aretino wrote. He was sending Titian's sketch to show that the portrait was an excellent likeness. He had borrowed a suit of armor so that every detail would be correct.

40

In the spring of 1541 D'Avalos received the Emperor at his court. Titian hurried to finish the General's picture, then took it to Milan. D'Avalos proudly showed it to his friends.

The masterpiece was damaged some years later and restored by other artists. It is no longer the great painting once so much admired in Milan.

D'Avalos Addressing His Soldiers

About 1541. (88" x 33⅝")

PRADO, MADRID. PHOTO ANDERSON

In four years Titian had lost five good friends and patrons. One after the other they had died; Alfonso, Urbino, Gonzaga, old Doge Gritti, and Cardinal de Medici. Perhaps he should have accepted the Cardinal's invitation to visit him in Rome. He might never have another chance to receive commissions from the Pope. But now it was too late. Ippolito de Medici had been poisoned.

He would miss his devoted patrons, but new important clients continued to knock at his door. Titian, just turned fifty, felt far from old; he could still work all day and entertain his friends at night. How he loved those evenings in his garden. As the sunset glow disappeared from the Cadore hills, the lagoon would be filled with the flickering lights of gondolas floating by. Sansovino was always there, boasting about his escapades with women, and Aretino, boisterous as ever, eating heartily and laughing at his own barbed jokes. He, like Titian, did not feel his age, although he was a few years older. He had worried about his graying beard, but had decided not to dye it. Titian had painted those gray hairs in the portrait Aretino had given to his publisher. How well Titian had understood his friend. Pietro Aretino was an important person who could afford a gold satin tunic and fur-trimmed purple velvet cloak. The gold chain around his neck was a present from the King of France. This was the man people called the "Scourge of Princes," willful, sensuous, and alert. "A terrible marvel," one friend called the portrait.

Every evening after the other guests had left, Titian, Aretino, and Sansovino talked until late at night. "The Triumvirate," they called themselves. Each was successful, and each admired the others' talent. They talked about the Doge's library Sansovino was designing, or Aretino's latest play. They discussed Titian's problem son, Pomponio. Aretino would send a sharp letter to the boy: "Pomponio, come home! It is time that you return from the country where there is no school," he wrote.

The Triumvirate worried about Titian's pension problems and talked a great deal about his recent troubles with the monks of Santo Spirito.

42

Pietro Aretino

About 1545. (40¼" x 33⅝")

FRICK COLLECTION, NEW YORK

On the island of Isola, just north of Venice, stood the church of Santo Spirito. Titian's painting of *Saint Mark Enthroned* had hung there for thirty years. Many of the monks who had commissioned it had died, but the younger monks decided to ask the same artist, now rich and famous, to paint a new altarpiece for their church. Only Titian could paint a picture of the Santo Spirito, or Holy Spirit, descending in rays of blinding light on worshipers below. It would illuminate the dark space above the altar just as *The Assumption* had brought light into the Frari church. The ceiling too must be illuminated with pictures of Bible stories; scenes which could be recognized from below.

Here was something Titian had not tried before. He would draw the figures as if they were being looked at from beneath. He sketched the figure of Abraham about to sacrifice his son; the giant Goliath slain by David, his head rolling on the ground; and Cain wielding a mighty club over his brother, Abel.

As soon as his sketches had been transferred to canvas, he started furiously to work. Assistants were busy putting the finishing touches on the picture of the Holy Spirit, while Titian completed the ceiling pictures.

The monks of Santo Spirito agreed that their new ceiling decorations were the best they had ever seen. Never had they believed that figures could be presented in this way. But the *Descent of the Holy Spirit* did not bring light into their church. Had it really been painted by the master? They had been told that assistants had been working on the picture. Or had it been damaged in the trip from Venice? Whatever the reason, Titian would not be paid until he produced another altarpiece.

Titian could not accept these terms. Aretino suggested that perhaps one of his influential clients might intervene and persuade the monks to change their minds. When the Pope's nephew, Cardinal Farnese, invited the artist to Bologna, where the Emperor was meeting with the Pope, Titian did not hesitate to accept the invitation.

44

Cain and Abel

1543–44. (110½" x 110½")

SANTA MARIA DELLA SALUTE, VENICE. PHOTO ANDERSON

The citizens of Bologna who passed Cardinal Farnese's house one spring day in 1543 were amazed to see a picture of the Pope leaning against the terrace wall. It was a striking likeness of the Holy Father they had seen borne on his chair through the streets of their city. One long-fingered bony hand rested on his money-bag, the other on the arm of his red velvet chair. His square beard made a white spot against his red velvet cape. His piercing black eyes looked out suspiciously from under a wrinkled brow.

The canvas was left to dry on the Cardinal's terrace, while Titian painted a portrait of his host. The Cardinal was delighted with the picture. Not only would he use his influence with the monks of Santo Spirito, he told the artist, but he would ask the Pope to settle a pension on Pomponio. The trip to Bologna had been worth while. But Titian did not know that the Cardinal was as tricky as his crafty uncle. One day, without a word to Titian, he left Bologna.

"The sudden departure of his Eminence caused me to spend a sleepless night," Titian wrote, after he returned to Venice. "The night would have been followed by a bad day," he continued, if the Cardinal's secretary had not assured him that the pension would be paid.

All through that summer Titian waited for the pension. He wrote to the Cardinal again. The portraits which had been so much admired had brought him fame but little money. He needed the money more than ever, as the monks of Santo Spirito were determined not to pay him for the damaged altarpiece.

"I beg your Reverend Lordship in remembrance of my services," he wrote, "to make [them] understand...so that they shall not have it in their power to ill-use me."

He wrote in vain. Pomponio never received a pension from the Pope and Titian was forced to paint another altarpiece.

Paul III

1543. (42" x 43")

NATIONAL MUSEUM, NAPLES. PHOTO ANDERSON

The workshop had never run so smoothly now that Orazio was old enough to help his father. Without him Titian could not have filled the orders which came to him that year of 1543. The *Assumption* altarpiece was not, perhaps, as majestic as the one in the Frari, but the artist Vasari had called it "the best modern painting in Verona." The Madonna altarpiece, painted in many sections, had been difficult, but in return Titian received a summer cottage on a hillside near Cadore. On one side he looked out on snow-capped mountains, and on the other, far below him, he saw Venice in a sea dotted with white sails. After a few days on this restful hilltop he would return refreshed and attack his paintings with new vigor.

He was anxious to finish his big picture of Christ brought before the people. It had been commissioned by a Dutch friend who lived in Venice. The wealthy merchant often called to see how the painting was progressing. He was amused that the bearded Pilate, who pointed haughtily toward the broken Christ, had the features of Aretino. He noted the play of light on the surging crowd. It was reflected in the armor of a soldier leaning on his shield, picked out the white turban of a Turkish soldier, the bald head of a red-robed bishop, and then burst out brilliantly on a young girl in white. The merchant recognized the lovely blonde. She had the features of Lavinia, Titian's beloved daughter.

Lavinia and Orazio were a comfort to their father. How different they were from their priest brother, Pomponio, who had already spent the income from the monastery given him by the Emperor. He might have received another pension if Titian had accepted Cardinal Farnese's invitation to come to Rome, but Aretino had approved of his friend's decision.

"You show how much...more distinguished Venice is than Rome," he wrote. But Cardinal Farnese was determined that the Venetian painter should visit the Holy City. In the fall of 1545, he arranged that the Duke of Urbino send a special escort to accompany Titian and his younger son to Rome.

Ecce Homo

1543. (95" x 142")

GEMALDEGALERIE, VIENNA

"Titian bids me adore the Duke," wrote Aretino to Urbino, "...in gratitude for the escort of seven riders, the payment of his journey...honors and presents and the hospitality of [the Pope's] palace which he was bid to treat as his own."

Titian was in Rome at last.

"Your Titian, or *our* Titian is here!" a cardinal wrote triumphantly to Aretino. "He has already seen so many fine antiques that he is filled with wonder." With the artist Vasari as his guide Titian toured the city. If only he had come twenty years before, he wrote Aretino; but although he was nearly sixty he would still learn from the great artists who had worked in Rome. He marveled at Michelangelo's monumental figures on the ceiling of the Pope's chapel and made sketches of Raphael's tapestries hanging on the walls.

Orazio set up a studio in the palace, and it was there that the Pope, old and shaky, posed for his portrait. Titian brushed in the bent figure huddled in his armchair. The old man tired easily. He did not pose again, but his two nephews came to the studio so that Titian could show them with their uncle. Cardinal Farnese, cold and aloof, stood behind the Pope's chair. His brother, Duke Ottavio, leaned forward to hear what his wily old uncle was about to say.

Duke Ottavio was now added to Titian's list of patrons. He commissioned a picture of a nude, the nymph Danae lying on a couch as she received a rain of gold from heaven. The picture was standing on an easel when Vasari brought Michelangelo to Titian's studio. The great artist grunted approval as he studied the glowing flesh tones, the rich red velvet couch cover and the radiant shower of gold coins.

"If the Venetian had learned to draw as well as paint," he told Vasari later, "he would have no equal."

When spring came Titian longed for the sea air of Venice. He was homesick for his friends and family. The Farneses had showered him with commissions, but the work had brought him little money. It was time for him to return to Biri Grande.

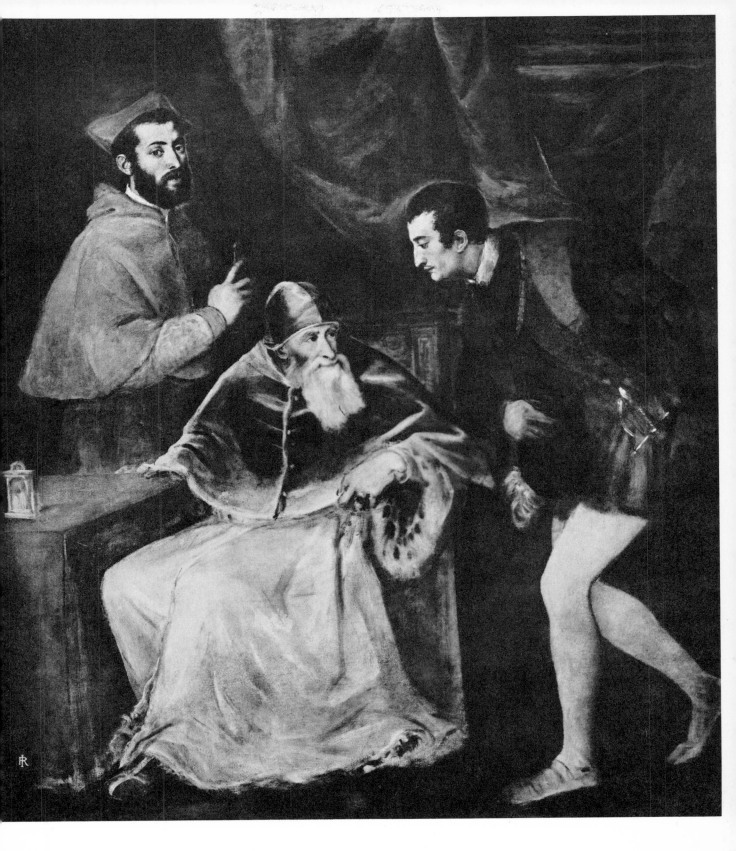

Paul III with His Nephews

1545–46. (83" x 68¾")

NATIONAL MUSEUM, NAPLES. PHOTO ANDERSON

It was good to be one of the Triumvirate again, talking about happenings in Venice and discussing family problems. It was time for Lavinia to be married. Her father must find her a proper husband and money for her dowry. Aretino suggested that Titian accept the Emperor's invitation to visit the court in Augsburg. Here was his chance to secure the dowry money.

In January 1548, Titian arrived in Augsburg. The ride across the Alps in midwinter had not been easy, even with the escort provided by the Emperor, but Aretino had wanted Titian to make the trip. Charles had just won a battle which made him master of most of Europe.

"You paint the Emperor," Aretino wrote to Titian, "on the horse he rode when he won the battle."

The sickly Emperor astride his charger looked proud and calm, but, seated in his armchair, his fur-lined mantle pulled around him, he looked old and sad. Titian painted the Emperor as he saw him, tortured by gout and burdened by responsibilities.

Titian stayed eight months in Augsburg, painting portraits of members of the court. In the spring Aretino sent him tragic news. Orsa Vecellio was dead.

"She was for you not only a sister, but a daughter, mother and friend," wrote Aretino. Lavinia's marriage would have to wait, for Titian needed his daughter to care for his busy household.

When Titian returned to Venice, thousands poured into his studio to offer sympathy, inquire about his trip, and look at the portraits of important people they had never seen. They admired a grieving Virgin, commissioned by the Emperor, which he planned to keep with him till he died. How often Charles talked of death, although he was only fifty! Titian at sixty-three still felt young. His face had aged, but his hands were vigorous as ever.

He picked up a brush and blocked in a portrait of himself, wearing a black skullcap, a fur-trimmed mantle, and the Emperor's gold chain around his neck. One capable hand rested on the table, the other on his knee. His strong face was intelligent and alert, the face of a great artist who was confident of his success.

Self-Portrait

About 1550. (38" x 29½")

STAATLICHEN MUSEEN, BERLIN. PHOTO STEINKOPF

Five years had passed since Titian returned from Rome, but he remembered vividly the great works of art which had impressed him; the stately buildings faced with columns, the antique statues, and the glorious paintings on the ceiling of the Pope's chapel. How skillfully Michelangelo had distorted the human figure to show dramatic action. How would he have painted the martyrdom of Saint Lawrence, Titian wondered, as he started to make sketches for another altarpiece. He placed the iron grill to which the saint was chained, at an angle so that the nude figure would be foreshortened. One arm was thrust back and upward toward a burst of light from heaven. He sketched a muscular figure in a turban, bending forward as he plunged a long fork into the saint's ribs; and another executioner on his knees, his torso twisted as he touched his torch to the blazing fire. He added more figures to the scene. A bearded man straining backward as he pulled the saint's shoulders, and armored soldiers carrying banners.

The canvas of Saint Lawrence stayed in the Biri Grande studio for five years before it was ready to hang in the Jesuit church in Venice. From time to time Titian would attack it with vigor. Many of the figures were as powerful as the ones he had admired in the Sistine Chapel, but even the great Michelangelo could not have flooded his canvas with such a dramatic light. Bright light from above fell on the saint's outstretched hand. Flames from the soldiers' torches played over the columns of the building in the background and picked out the stately form of an antique statue standing on an enormous pedestal.

Titian painted furiously. Then one day he turned the canvas to the wall. Once again he had been called to Augsburg; this time to paint portraits of the Emperor's son.

The Martyrdom of Saint Lawrence

1550–59. (197½″ x 110″)

GESUITI CHURCH, VENICE. PHOTO ANDERSON

In the fall of 1550 Titian set off on the long, cold journey across the mountains. He hoped that he would be rewarded for his trip. Charles's son, Philip, would soon replace his father. It was important to have the future Emperor for a patron.

Titian was shocked when he met the Emperor's son. Philip, like his father, was pale and sickly. His lower lip was thick and prominent, his bulging blue eyes heavy. Titian wondered if a truthful portrait of this pallid prince would appeal to the English Queen, whom Charles had chosen for Philip's bride. Queen Mary was waiting impatiently to see a likeness of the Spanish prince who hoped to win her hand.

Philip had little time to pose. Titian made a sketch of his nervous sitter dressed in royal robes. From this sketch he painted portraits of the Prince, one in somber black and another in resplendent armor. This was the portrait the Spanish ambassador took to England. Queen Mary was enchanted by the picture. She was charmed by Philip's wide brow and the subtle coloring in his face. She admired his elegant legs, encased in tight white stockings, and his aristocratic hands, one of which rested on his sword, the other on his plumed helmet beside him. She was flattered that this prince, ten years younger, had chosen her for his bride.

Titian wrote to Aretino about his life in Augsburg, "this torrid zone where we are all dying of the cold." The Emperor had received him cordially, had asked about Aretino, and had even hinted that the Pope was thinking of making his friend a cardinal. Titian hoped to return to Venice soon. Philip had already returned to Spain, and the Emperor planned to move on to Innsbruck. But before Charles said good-by to Titian, he wanted to discuss the painting he had commissioned.

King Philip II

1550. (76" x 44")

PRADO, MADRID. PHOTO ANDERSON

Charles looked gloomier than ever as he told Titian about his decision to retire to a monastery. He wanted a picture of the Last Judgment which he could contemplate until he died. God and Christ would sit enthroned in heaven. Charles and his family, wrapped in shrouds, would beg for mercy. The Virgin, draped in darkest blue, would stand below, pleading for the saints who surged in a semicircle of clouds beneath her.

Titian made sketches for the picture before he returned to Venice. Charles looked at them a long time. He saw himself kneeling in fervent prayer, his crown beside him. His wife knelt behind him. Philip's pale, anxious face showed above the shrouded figure of his sister. He marveled at the vigor of the figures below. He recognized Moses, holding up a tablet of the law, and Noah holding a model of the ark.

There were many parties for Titian when he returned to Venice in the spring, and more work waiting for him in his studio. Some days he painted vigorously, but other days he could not touch a canvas. Perhaps that was why Charles had written asking if he was dead. His ambassador hastened to reply. "Titian is alive and well," he wrote, "and working on the Emperor's canvas. The other picture...of the grieving Virgin...has not been sent as he has not yet been sent the measurements."

There were other reasons why the picture was not ready. Titian was filling a commission for Charles's son and painting pictures for the Doge. Three years went by before the paintings were shipped to Brussels, and with them a letter from the artist. He had not received the income from the land grants offered by the Emperor:

58

"I am straitened for means, having been ill in health and having betrothed my daughter," Titian wrote. The picture of the grieving Virgin reflected his own grief, he continued: "My supplications...find expression in the record of her image which now comes before your majesty."

The Last Judgment (La Gloria)

1554. (136¾" x 95")

PRADO, MADRID. PHOTO ANDERSON

Titian never forgot how beautiful Lavinia looked that June day in 1555 when she was married to the young man he had chosen as her husband. He painted her that year in her white satin wedding dress. Pearls were wound in her hair, pearls hung from her ears, and a string of pearls circled her white neck. Two gold bracelets studded with jewels were fastened around her wrists and in her hand she held a little flag. Her clear dark eyes, so like her father's, looked out calmly from the picture.

How he would miss his only daughter, who had cared so capably for his household! He was comforted that Orazio was managing the workshop. He needed comfort, for Pomponio had gone from bad to worse.

"You ought to have denied bread to your son," Aretino had once told his friend. Titian did not forget those words. He wrote to the Duke of Mantua, asking him to transfer Pomponio's pension to a Vecellio nephew.

"My son," he wrote, "has not much inclination for the church."

Every day Titian was troubled by money problems. Lavinia's dowry had been paid at last, but he still had not received any money from the Emperor's land grants. Nor could he expect any money from the Doge until he had finished an enormous canvas commissioned by the government council.

60

Lavinia as a Bride

1555. (40½" x 34")

GEMALDEGALERIE, DRESDEN. PHOTO ALINARI

Titian remembered the day long ago when the captain of the Venetian fleet who had lost a battle against the Turks was led in chains to the government prison. He remembered, too, how twenty-two years later that same captain marched in state to the government palace to be crowned as Doge. Now thirty years after Doge Grimani's death, the government council decided to honor his memory with a painting.

Titian set to work on the huge canvas. Doge Grimani, wearing his gold ducal cape over shining armor, had fallen to his knees, dazzled by the vision of a cross held by a beautiful woman symbolizing faith. Saint Mark, his lion by his side, turned from his book to gaze in wonder at the heavenly sight. Two soldiers stood behind the Doge, one enraptured, the other turned away. A page in red knelt beside his master, holding the ducal cap. In the distance the Venetian fleet lay at anchor in the blue lagoon.

Titian's work was constantly interrupted. Those calls from Philip's ambassador were annoying. He had written to Philip many times, telling him that his paintings would soon be ready. How he missed Aretino's eloquent pen! It hardly seemed possible that his friend had gone. He had died so suddenly, only a few days after a gay party, when Pietro, laughing at his own joke had fallen over backward in his chair. Many rejoiced that the "Scourge of Princes" had received the punishment he deserved, but Titian and Sansovino missed the third member of the Triumvirate. Aretino would have advised him on how to procure the pension money. Would he ever receive the income from the land grants, now that Charles was dead? He would mention it to Philip when he sent his paintings. He hurried to finish them while his assistants worked on the Doge Grimani picture. He had many good assistants now: the dyers' son, nicknamed Tintoretto, the Greek boy whom people called El Greco, and the youth from Verona who was known in Venice as Veronese.

The Doge Grimani painting was not finished in Titian's lifetime. Pupils completed it after the artist's death. Today its golden radiance lights up one of the dark rooms in the Doge's Palace.

Votive Picture of Doge Grimani (La Fede)

1550–70. (144" x 197½")

DOGE'S PALACE, VENICE. PHOTO ANDERSON

"I have now completed the two 'poesies'," Titian wrote Philip in the summer of 1559. "When your majesty wishes to have them," he continued, "simply command me to whom they shall be sent."

He had worked hard on these mythological scenes for Philip. And there was no Orazio to help him in the workshop. His son had gone to Milan to try to collect the land-grant income.

Titian wondered why Philip, who was as fervently religious as his father, should order pictures of nude gods and goddesses. He knew the King would like these pictures of stories about Diana, particularly the one of the bathing nymphs surprised by the hunter Acteon. Diana, her arms upraised, was trying to cover herself with a filmy robe, another nymph pulled a curtain, and a third crouched shyly on the edge of the fountain. Light flickering through the trees bathed the figures in vibrating light.

Titian wrote Philip that the other pictures he had ordered would soon be ready: "I will put all the knowledge God has given me into the work," he wrote, and hoped that His Majesty would continue to employ him, "so long as I can use my limbs." A few weeks later Titian wrote again. He had just received a letter from Milan. Orazio had been seriously wounded by his host, who had tried to get his money. Would Philip please order the arrest of this man who had tried to murder Titian's beloved son, "for if Orazio were dead, I also would be dead myself from grief."

Orazio did not die. He returned to Venice some months later to find the Biri Grande studio busier than ever. Titian was working hard, but tired easily. He felt older since his recent trip to Cadore, where he attended his brother's funeral. How long ago it seemed since he and Francesco had come to Venice to work in Zuccato's studio! Perhaps it was money worries that tired him. Letter after letter he wrote to Philip asking if the "poesies" had arrived or why he had not been paid. He complained to Philip's ambassador, who gave him little sympathy.

"Titian being old is somewhat covetous," wrote the ambassador from Venice.

Diana and Acteon

1559. (75" x 81¾")

EARL OF ELLESMERE COLLECTION, ON LOAN TO THE
NATIONAL GALLERY OF SCOTLAND, EDINBURGH

Philip's ambassador reported on the progress of his paintings. Titian was finishing the religious pictures. The artist had already written Philip that *The Last Supper* was completed, "a work which is perhaps the most important that I ever did," he wrote; but he added, "as till now I have not had the slightest payment for the numerous works which I have finished." Was this the reason Titian would not let the picture leave his studio?

"I shall consider this the true cause," Philip's ambassador told his master, "but I shall still try to obtain it...for though Titian is old, he works and can still work."

Visitors to his studio watched fascinated as the white-bearded artist, now nearly eighty, attacked his canvas, applying thick strokes of color, then smearing them with his thumb or with the handle of his brush. His friend Vasari, just arrived from Rome, remarked on Titian's change in style; "These last [paintings] are done with broad coarse strokes," he wrote. "They should not be examined near at hand." The recent portrait of himself, though roughly painted, was an excellent likeness. He had grown thinner since he had painted himself fifteen years before. His expression was sadder but serene. Brush in hand, he stood ready to take on new commissions.

Many commissions were finished by his pupils. He was becoming more and more dependent on Orazio. He must arrange to leave a fortune to this devoted son. It would help if he listed deductions on his income tax. The Biri Grande house had been a financial loss, Titian wrote; his country cottage a mere shabby hut. He never even mentioned his salary from the government or the pension from the Emperor. Later he wrote to the council and to Philip, asking them to transfer this income to his son.

He felt happier now that he had provided for Orazio's future. He still did not feel his age. It was hard to believe that he and Sansovino were over eighty. For the past few weeks Sansovino had been ill. Then suddenly, in the fall of 1570, the second member of the Triumvirate died. Titian was broken hearted.

Self-Portrait

About 1565. (34" x 25¾")

PRADO, MADRID. PHOTO ANDERSON

Titian had been deeply saddened by the loss of his two best friends, and Lavinia's sudden death had been a crushing blow. Life seemed less and less important. Even the recent news that the Turkish fleet had been defeated did not excite him, although the rest of Venice celebrated madly. Philip wrote to him about a painting honoring this victory of the Spanish and Venetian fleets. He enclosed sketches by a Spanish artist showing what he wanted; a dull, pompous picture of Philip holding up his newborn son before an angel of victory hovering above him.

Titian dreaded taking on a big commission and suggested that the artist who had made the sketches should also paint the picture. But Philip would have only Titian.

Orazio wondered if his father no longer worried about financial problems. Commissions no longer interested him. He had started a *Pietà* as a present for the Frari monks, who had agreed that he could be buried in their church. Thoughts of death were constantly in Titian's mind as he painted this picture of the dead Christ on his Mother's lap. On one side Mary Magdalene rushed forward, arms outstretched, and on the other Saint Jerome had fallen to his knees. His bearded face, turned in profile, had Titian's strong, sharp features.

All through the steaming summer of 1576 Titian painted. He refused to leave the city even when the plague struck Venice. Every day bodies were piled in carts and taken to the country, for the government forbade any burials in the city. Then, on August 27, Venetians learned that Titian of Cadore was dead. The council met and voted that his body he buried in the Frari church as a tribute to their greatest artist.

Grief-stricken Orazio followed his father's body to the church. Two days later he too was dead.

The *Pietà* remained in the Biri Grande studio until it was completed by one of Titian's pupils. Then before it was taken to the church, the artist wrote an inscription at the bottom of the picture:

"THAT WHICH TITIAN LEFT UNFINISHED, PALMA REVERENTLY COMPLETED AND DEDICATED TO THE WORK OF GOD."

Pietà

1573–76. (138¾" x 153¾")

ACCADEMIA, VENICE. PHOTO ALINARI

ACKNOWLEDGEMENTS

I wish to thank Mrs. Nina Longobardi for her kindness in allowing me to use the library in the American Academy in Rome, and Professor Dr. Ulrich Middledorf for graciously permitting me to read in the Kunsthistorischen library in Florence.

BIBLIOGRAPHY

Basch, Victor, *Titien*. Albin Michel, Paris, 1926

Bensusan, S. L., *Titian*. Stokes, New York, 1908

Checchi, Dario, *Titian*. Translated from the Italian by Nora Wydenbruck, John Calder, London, 1957

Crowe and Cavalcaselle. *Titian*, His Life and Times. John Murray, London, 1877

Fischel, Oscar, *Tizian*. Meister Gemalde. Deutsche Verlags-Anstalt. Stuttgart, Berlin, Leipzig

Fosca, François, *Titian*, Translated by Lucy Norton, William Heinemann, Ltd., London, 1955

Gilbert, Josiah, *Cadore, or Titian's Country*. Longmans, Green and Co., London, 1869

Gronau, Georg, *Titian*, Charles Scribner's Sons. New York, 1904

Hadeln, Detlev, Baron von, *Titian's Drawings*. Macmillan and Co., London, 1927

Horticq, Louis, *La Jeunesse de Titien*, Paris, 1919

Jameson, Mrs. *The House of Titian, in Studies, Stories and Memoirs*. Houghton, Mifflin Co., Boston, 1885

Lafenestre, Georges. *La Vie et l'Oeuvre de Titien*. Societé Française d'Editions d'Art. L. Henry May, Paris

Mitchell, D. M. *Bound Together*. Charles Scribner's Sons, New York, 1884

Pope, Arthur. *Titian's Rape of Europa*. Harvard University Press, 1960

Ricketts, Charles, S. *Titian*. Methuen and Co. Ltd., 1910

Riggs, Arthur S. *Titian the Magnificent, and the Venice of his day*. Bobbs Merrill, New York, 1946

Tietze, Hans, *Titian, the Paintings and Drawings*. Phaidon Press, Ltd., London, 1950

Titian, with an introduction and notes by James Laver. Faber and Faber, London, 1950

Titian, Text by Theodore Rousseau, Jr. Harry N. Abrams, Inc. New York, 1955

INDEX